BIG RIG

Written by Dale Wildman
Illustrated by Bill Dickson

Cassie the cat lives in SW Ohio, and allows Dale Wildman and his three children to live with her.

Dedicated to Bill Vida, who let me ride in his truck.

© 2006. Published by Journey Stone Creations, LLC.
All rights reserved. Printed in China by Global PSD.
Little Gems is an imprint of Journey Stone Creations, LLC
First print run, 2006

ISBN# 1-59958-007-1
Please visit our web site for other great titles.
www.jscbooks.com

He even wanted it more than a trip to the zoo where he could see the monkeys monkey around on Monkey Island, which always made him laugh out loud and which was the second-most something he ever wanted, even though he'd already done it a few times.

    The first-most something Livingston Brumble wanted was a ride in his daddy's truck. Mr. Brumble drove a big, BIG truck, that he parked in the long gravel driveway next to Livingston's house. His mom called his dad's truck a semi-truck, but his dad just called it a Big Rig. So that's what Livingston called it, too.

Livingston knew his dad used his truck to haul all kinds of things, from ladders to furniture to machinery. "Everything including the kitchen sink," Mr. Brumble always said, cheerily. Livingston couldn't imagine who would want a truck full of kitchen sinks, but that's what his dad always said, anyway.

What Livingston COULD imagine was riding in the Big Rig with his dad, looking down on all the cars and pulling on the strap that sounded the truck horn, the one that made the super loud 'WOOOOO-WOOOOO' sound. That would be awesome, Livingston thought.

But Livingston's dad was a long-haul trucker, which meant he used his truck to haul things a long way away, and was often gone for days at a time. Livingston's mom didn't want Livingston to be gone from home for very long, so she always said the same thing. "I'm sorry, Livingston, it's too far and you're too young to be gone so long. Maybe when you're older."

Livingston knew his mom was just being his mom, but he couldn't help feeling disappointed. Still, he thought maybe if he could just ride in SOME truck, he might feel better.

So he went to the firehouse, and asked the firefighters for a ride. And one day when there weren't any fires, they let Livingston ride with them around the block. They even turned the siren on for a few seconds.

Livingston thought that was pretty cool, but it just wasn't the same. He thanked them for the ride, but he still wanted to ride with his dad.

The next day, he saw a brown UPS™ truck pull up to his house, to deliver some curtains to Mrs. Brumble. "Maybe it would be fun to ride in *that* truck," he thought, and ran out to ask if he could. "Well, I can't let you do that," said the driver. "But I'll let you look inside for a minute."

Livingston looked in eagerly, but all he saw was a bunch of shelves and a small, crowded space. There weren't even any seats. Actually, to Livingston, the inside of the UPS truck just looked like a big closet, though of course he didn't say so. He thanked the driver for letting him look, but it just wasn't the same as the Big Rig. Livingston walked slowly back to the house, sadder than ever.

To make things even worse, Livingston's school had just announced that Friday would be "Take-Your-Son-to-Work Day" for all the boys in Livingston's class. The girls had already had their "go to work" day, and now every boy would get to go with his dad...except Livingston.

Now Livingston wanted to ride with his dad more than ever. But his mother just shook her head.

Livingston hoped Friday would never come, but it did, and a right bright, sunny day it was. When Livingston got to school, his teacher, Mrs. Lohr, told the boys she had good news. "All your dads will be here at ten o'clock this morning," she said, "to take you with them to work."

Everyone cheered, except Livingston. He had never felt so lonely in his life. While the other kids laughed and talked all around him, Livingston just sat in his seat, miserable, with his chin in his hands, and looked out the window at the lawn of green grass that stretched all the way out to the school road.

At ten o'clock exactly, there was a knock at the door. Mrs. Lohr went to answer it, and in came all the dads, who stood in a line at the front of the class.

"Is everybody ready?" Mrs. Lohr asked the class. "Yes? Then let's see..." All at once she stopped talking and looked at the row of waiting dads. "I do believe we're missing somebody," she said.

Suddenly, Livingston heard the loud, long blast of a truck horn. He looked out the window to see where it came from, and ... could it be?

Livingston and all the other kids crowded over by the schoolroom windows. Out on the road, next to the school lawn, was Mr. Brumble's big red truck. Livingston's dad was in it, and he was yelling for Livingston! "Come on, Livingston!" he hollered, waving his hand out the open truck window.

Livingston looked in astonishment at the smiling Mrs. Lohr. "That's right, Livingston," she said. "Your mom and dad called the school and arranged for your dad to pick you up this way. He has a short haul today, right here in town, and you're going with him!"

Everybody went outside, and cheered as Livingston ran across the lawn to his dad's Big Rig. Mr. Brumble opened the big truck's passenger side door, leaned over to grab Livingston's hand, and pulled him right up and into the cab.

"Once before we go, Livingston!" said his dad, and a laughing Livingston grabbed on to the horn strap and pulled with all his might.

"WOOOOOO-WOOOOOO!!"